Copyright © 2024 by F. S. Withers
Cover © 2024 by Elliott Sharpe @spogart on Instagram
All rights reserved. No part of this book may be reproduced in any manner whatsoever without written permission except in the case of brief quotations embodied in critical articles and reviews.

First Printing, 2024

QUASARS & QUININE

to everyone i have loved enough to weave into text,

to those who narrowly escaped my stanzas,

and all the great loves i haven't met yet

FORWORD

Years ago, probably around the time "nyc" was written, I had a dream that I was sitting at the kitchen table holding a coffee cup. In it swirled an entire galaxy. It might have been the Milky Way, or maybe it was Andromeda. I had this feeling like if I drank it I would get high, like it was some hallucinogenic substance I was preparing to ingest, a journey I would embark on. I don't remember what it tasted like going down, but it felt insurmountably heavy to keep inside. It's nice to get things out.

In music theory, a "leitmotif" (German, meaning "leading motive") is a recurring musical phrase. In literature, a leitmotif becomes to a piece of work what the tune of a chorus is to a song: something repeated, a fixture, an exclamation point or an underline. In this passion project, I've included plenty of patterns and callbacks and recurrent words or phrases, bite-sized leitmotifs for you to listen to. I want you to ask yourself what the point of it all is and sit with me in those moments. I want you to think about them as if they are a room in my home that I welcome you into again and again, where we spend time, where you familiarize yourself with the furniture, what matches and what stands out.

Although I live in a studio apartment now, there are other rooms in this metaphorical home. They are rooms I would welcome you to see in theory, but I can't show them to you right now. I am allowed to keep things in, because there will always be too much to say and not enough time or space to say it. I hope you walk through my home as a guest who understands nuance. Maybe someday I will have time to write about all the things I care about. For now, thank you for coming and I hope you enjoy your visit. Would you like some coffee? Tea? A drink? Do you take cream, sugar? Ice? Tonic?

nyc
2015

a collective breath as the subway moves
some soles have been riding for so long they don't flinch

prism #9
3/10/17

red

you call me cherry

you say it's because my kisses

are the „cherry on top" of the relationship

to me you are a teal

like the turquoise earrings i got for you at the brass armadillo in arizona

freckled like your cheeks

framed oval with curled sterling as if they were tiny parlor mirrors

like in the bathroom when you said you learned to like your nose because people said it was beautiful

you are teal like the dress you wore when we painted your bedroom gold

your hands encased, preserved

you deserve it

you are gold

and i am red

like henna

thick and ugly but beautiful as it oxidizes

give me time. breathe into me

so i don't need to come up for air.

we are like clams

in the ocean

blue

and learning how to be vulnerable

opening each other's mouths as we kiss in the shower

your makeup bleeding against my cheek as i bite your lip and pull your hair

red

dripping wet

cooperative when pulled

and you like it that way.

you talked about thursday night

i told you i loved you as you sat on my lap

we were covered in plastic wrap

my whole body felt like it was shaking

my heart beating faster than my adenosine receptors could be blocked

like coffee, you are an addiction

and you told me once if you were a neurotransmitter you would want to be dopamine

and i said i'd be serotonin

and after i say i love you

you tell me you love me too

and we believe each other

because it is the truth.

time moves slow when i'm with you

and when i close my eyes and cry

i smile

because i can see every color

spread out across a calendar that says july

when we first exchanged glasses, yours rose-colored

mine like the sun

round lenses like we didn't belong

trying to see from a different perspective

my face was red like a tomato

(i only like them cold)

blushing

the color of your lips

your pupils like the kind of abyss

i would want to stare into

i could drown in you

tangled up in blue

and never need to breathe again.

untitled

4/13/17

my coworker told me today

we lose one percent of our ability to feel physical sensation

from the age of eighteen on.

although i don't believe that claim,

i listened to her speak.

she said that's why old folks always fall

they can't feel the ground like they did when they were eighteen

feet in the grass

young, vulnerable

learning to love

and growing up to ruin the economy and blame it on us

because we feel too much

i think about my mother and i worry about the number of times she has fallen,

her memory only a guiding force against the small cracks and bumps

her feet still eighteen

her body numb

i think about the number of times she didn't tell me

because she thought i had it worse

apologetic on behalf of a generation who gave me trump

and alcoholism

foreclosed homes and bankruptcy

political correctness a guise for basic respect neglected

but i am living off student loan refunds

and she is living in a motel room with social security

she keeps the cream by the door

because it's cooler

and she pours it in her coffee in the morning as she prepares to look on craigslist for openingsand when i ask her to come over and have a cup she says no, i'm too busy, she'd rather leave me be

when i was a child

before i knew what adults were capable of

i used to think the world was really black and white in the nineteen fifties

and dinosaurs must have existed around the same time.

i didn't know that other children

could grow into adults

and with an autograph take my rights away

when i was a child

i used to lay in bed with my mother

and make sure i was the first to say „i love you"

because i didn't want her to die before i did

and maybe if i said it before she did, i would go first

i didn't want to hurt

i had too many nerve endings

i wonder how much she feels

womanism
2018

"i'm still here" she says
her voice echoes in atoms
in the the doldrums of spacetime as it expands and contracts
but you, stuck in your vacuum,
have made no effort to hear
because she's not on your wavelength
do you think yourself a nebulaic anomaly? elemental travesty
she, too, has observable light
you're just choosing not to see

guilty pleasure
12/18/19

when i was 21 my roommate suggested that maybe if i wanted to save money i should stop buying cage free organic eggs

i don't hold it against him because i said and did things back then that hurt him, too

like when i didn't want to eat a croissant he made because it had too many calories and i was trying to look like someone who didn't do cocaine

and then later i heard him throwing up in the shower

his bones too weak to support the weight of the world

we criticize ourselves and each other

crack ourselves open

on medium heat

we allow resentment to boil in a saucepan

we let the shame steep

like tea

i sometimes feel condescended by yogi brand

(i feel condescended by all brands because they are a part of something i didn't ask to participate in, and now i'm at the grocery store trying to decide how i personally can reduce the amount of children working in sweatshops when i am not the one who put them there)

(pass go, collect $5 salary, spend it on yogi brand tea)

when yogi teas tell me to spread light and love it is no different from the man on the train telling me i'd be prettier if i smiled

in retaliation i buy my green tea moisturizer so that the laugh lines take longer to etch themselves into my face i think it is so funny that we feel so shameful

for enjoying things

isn't it nice to have somewhere to put all that love?

we have to spend time

doing things we enjoy doing

when i was 23 my roommate chastised me for eating so much annie's organic macaroni & cheese

but i was broke and in college same as them

wiping the blood from my nose trying to learn how to eat again

trying to learn how to stop drinking

or at least find a better guilty pleasure

but she was sad, too

i remember i showed her a kpop music video someone had showed to me at a party and got her into kpop

and then i made fun of her for being so into kpop

and now i am 26 and it is 3 a.m. and watching BTS on jimmy fallon

is one of the few things that's made me laugh this week

my age
4/2/20

i still remember the smell of hot dust settled in cars

rolling steady down highways in the rain while the jets played

rocking sturdy on the ferry looking at the sunlight scattered across the waves

that lake was so deep you could sink a house in it

shallow by the bay

brown murky question mark

tadpoles in puddles

the smell of pulling up. sound of gravel

red mud caked in the tires

holiday house parked right on the golf course

holiday cabin made live-in way back when

when i was my age

i would sit up in the nook drawing on printer paper big long rectangular sheets

grandpa was a CPA

i would sleep upstairs in the hallway overlooking everyone

looking up to everyone

when i slept the wizard of oz watched me

when i went downstairs i could smell the curry

or the wet cement of the cellar

but i'll never forget the dead moth i kept in a glass coffin

because i thought it was beautiful
or the brushstrokes on the ceiling of the yellow room
hornets by the window
hand picked fresh raspberries
homemade ice cream after yahtzee
home away from home
spearmint and sunscreen in my nose
the fourth of july
over to old la pointe
under sunshine and flowers
and wood in the woodstove
orange rolls for breakfast, limeade at dinner
and an egg sandwich on the way out
buttery and perfect
smörkranz on a platter
from a family
on an island
when things weren't so heavy

erde
7/4/20

the earth is full of unshed tears, spinning, trapped in a quincunx of contained chaos

they say space is a vacuum but i think if you listen hard enough you can hear

strauss's screaming violins

pulsetempo of a million heartbeats alive and dead

echoing in the caverns of yesterday-tomorrow

merging with everything-nothing

all of the you's and i's, possessing and unpossessing

comparing ourselves to each other when there wasn't ever anything to compare us to

theories of relativity

merging ourselves until we are one, existing in the in-between

the yes and throwing out the no but

frankenstein's monstrous ill-formed society of warmongers put together on hegemony and held up in hedonism,

is it all that bad in the grandiose scheme of things, though, huh?

we let the dark matter engulf the light

the problem is light just don't move fast enough sometimes

anyway, not all things dark are damaged

there must be a whole lotta bright inside a supermassive black hole

this sort of lighterman's hitch tying time to space, well

that's an approximation by proxy

in the paradox of is and isn't

soul prosthesis

is

it does the job whether it's real or not

1:21:21
8/28/20

time may be fleeting but night is forgiving

space makes me greedy but daylight is promising

sitting here speaking not really believing

but when i hold her she says, "dear, mind your breathing"

and i still don't know if i'm waking or sleeping

maybe i'm attempting to be lucid dreaming

flying through ceilings and loving and bleeding

and feeding this me that sometimes is receding

reminders remember the things you were needing

and pain cements beauty in hearts that keep beating

2:22 (SGT)
8/28/20

I see you speak in colors,
Wanna open you up like a kaleidoscope
Take you apart in shapes scream fate like the way pupils dilate
You, the center of gravity tugging tight on light spectrums to your center, me like an iris, surrounding you, warmth and radiation, soft and dangerous, bringing us
Home to a dimension where ions collide, pressed together like atoms, molecular kiss

paradise
9/25/20

thinking about germany more often than not

how i lost my heart in heidelberg

in a castle

in some hills

by a river

in europe the country looks so much wider the cities more condensed

history than we will ever know

because here in our land we've erased it

rolled vellum over soil and threw away the calf

not that europe is better

just that sometimes waking up on a bus the clouds looked bigger and the moon loomed closer

drenching massive mountains

the austrian countryside reminding me why goethe wrote

and in italy that morning i saw why trees grow

i think about sharing that umbrella with brittany in the rain getting lost together

wetter weather

stepping on ruins and

walking up stairs

looking into a volcano and seeing only sand

i think now i understand

the significance of sleepless nights spent wandering berlin sitting on the sidewalk with strangers until sunrise

we played games and drank wine

or in hamburg when

hamburg is another story

we love you, samanta

i think back to the first time not berlin or munich but darmstadt

innard city

that's where i reached inside myself and planted something that could grow

tiny gardens with berries whose names i did not know

learned the word in a tongue i once knew

like when i asked the father of the household

— who never let me du —

Sie, i said, what are you thinking about

in that house that felt like home the way they always did

he was looking out the window maybe seeing goethe's moonlight

and he said something back which i do not remember

but i do recall the slump of his shoulders and the wist welling up in his eyes as he told me something as if it should be a secret

and i forgot the words but i never forgot the feeling

i think it was something about youth

suite d'ors
12/12/2020

they wrote poems and songs about me

sometimes without ever having touched me

like knowing me is enough

on the couch one of them asked if he

could ask me a question i said jokingly You Just Did and when he asked another

i was thrown off but he assured me he hadn't really been interested

until he heard me speak

second question yes third question no left him unsatisfied but i steeped in my apathy like forgotten tea

i didn't ask but he brought me beer from his brewery every other week

like collateral for the kisses i gave freely and with no heat

i keep them simmering on low make them beg to be boiled

my roommate says bitterly "frankie i don't know how you get all these people to fall in love with you, it's like you charm them"

like looks aren't enough

at least, mine aren't

my roommate is beautiful

but i've got a glowing personality

and an inability to get any closer

i'm all talk

under the covers when all i really want to do is get up and walk

the waxing is poetic but i'm waning

efface withers

loved but not loving

lover but not plural

everybody's got my number but nobody's pulled my card

maybe if i try

to draw or sing or write

the way they did like documenting their perception of me would ensure

my gentle capture like wings held mid-flight

then i'll find reasons to understand

why they were right

VOICE
12/9/21

something i have noticed is

in 3D he sings the notes longer,

draws them out like he can stretch time

across his elastic voice

all my life i have never been able to find a song

which measures itself not in beats but in ticks

hands gripping clockwise breath transcending like gentle breeze across the universe

seconds do not adhere to signatures

but we can try to leave our mark

list

2/1/21

Different types of tears:

Tears that prick like chlorine

Tears that flow hot wet and unending

Tears that leave me gasping

Tears my eyes hang onto

Saltwater mascara, liquid magnets

Tears that get stuck in my throat

Trying to explain/can't make a sound

The world keeps spinning

71% tears

Beautiful vulnerable tears, laughing and holding you vice-tight tears

Kissing you softly curtain-eyed tears, wine tears that leave stains the next day

Cracking on a city bus tears, sunset sidewalk tears

Empathy for atoms

Feeling for concrete and glass

Feeling for leaves

Feet in the grass

Tears that fall like rain

Leave room for things to grow

cell shade/window pain
2/8/21

i see noise

no not like loud, not sound

like static

thought i could see atoms (never eves)

lore said maybe i can

the way i always describe it is

an old television set, or a film or digital photograph

speckled with tiny buzzing pin-pricks

myriad shade

overlaid like a filter on my visible light spectrum

maybe it is subjective but everything is

that's what i remind myself when i don't feel like

i've been told i'm an artist

i've been told as an artist i can render colors well

i think the opposite is true. i cannot render colors as they are

i can take them, transverse and inverse them,

change them and wring them out and twist them into something new

the moment is blue

or maybe it's green

sun streaming in through large windows draped in crimson

sheer, not clear

and in this moment i am more stirred than shaken

more dream than terror

even though i'm still there

i am also here

both things can exist at once

like how when i was a child i would peer through my fingers

looking at my skin and the vision within

see-through

my two eyes allowing me to see different perspectives

in one cognition

ignition repetition fruition

working memory R.E.M. indigo skies indigo girls mazzy stars like diamonds hung in a desert curtain

i can do this i am okay

i am away/i am aware

i am staying/i am awake

i want to get better

i am impatient

i want to take

i want to give

so i think i'll wait

and see

dizzy
2/14/21

constant comet
centrifugal force
honest dancer
the sunsets you send
days so long and nights without end
meticulously-arranged breakfast in bed
gorgeous aura
palette of blues and greys
every inch of skin a canvas
diptych dripping afternoon sun and fairy lights
sweat and tears
though you say i am not indebted
i think i owe you this poem
because you have written so much about me
i didn't know what it was to be amused
on parle, on écoute
comme si on s'aimait
j'adore, je voudrais
we sing the magnetic fields in strings and keys while you put on a kettle
boiling words/ginsberg howls
trapped in time trapped in space
trapped in a cage, a song, a place,

what's in a name,

lore,

you are a story i can't wait to read

every page

eternally unfinished

we are greedy

we talk like immortals running out of time

desperately exchanging Rorschach theories of the universe

you've developed a new molecule

and you assure me we can see disruptions in the spectrum

we watch them like clouds on your ceiling

fractured fractals to the fourth dimension

rippling depths

you are a soft specter

you overflow

you love like you will die

and live like you haven't

masticating media

chewing on lemongrass from your fridge

bottom shelf on the right, careful containercapricorn moon

my feelings are a locked file cabinet

and yours an ancient archive

memories an ocean so deep

mirror eyes, you know what it is to drown

black hole focus, magic potions, getting seasick when we kiss

but that's my favorite type of sex

because you have to close your eyes.

you assure me it's good

that nobody else has done this to you

i am only a little surprised

you can't see how broken i am

when i tell you i'm not complete yet.

t rial and

error

i love us so much i feel scared

you show me what it is like to feel cared for

you show me what it is like to feel seen

so i'd rather blindfold you

and tell you what to do

so you don't have time to tell me what you've deduced

a year ago when we were introduced i

wanted to exchange art and

(now we are)

with one word i predicted our future

manifesting off-chances

having off-days

i may be flighty but

you are the sort of cage i do not feel the need to escape

is-n't
3/14/21

is   n't
    let me tell you
      the difference between
being human
     and
        human being
it
is
the first language they teach you
         it
         isn't
a language you're allowed to speak
it was his fault for being born naked
    when he should have been
       draped in silk and taffeta
that's what   s e p a r a t e s
them   and   us

so they took him from his home
and they gave him a new name
and they buried him in exoticism
     they did not bury him at all

    the thing about language is

               what's in a name?

    it carries power

        not in letters but in

                lips teeth and tongue

    powdered and painted with purloined gold

    it is a shape

    it is a mould

               it was built broken

               chipped and peeling

                  stolen and sold

    it is a play

    it is a stage

                   it is a script

                   it is a cage

    it is a game   only some win

    it is the shaky foundation

            of an apartment in berlin

    it   it

    is   isn't

    colonization   discovery

it	it
is	isn't
imperialism	expansion

it	it
is	isn't
changing	over

	community	
it		not
	is	

for Angelo Soliman
for May Ayim
for stellende gemeinschaften
and for us

photosynthesis/time kisses and tells
3/20/21

i am tired of speaking in exhausted metaphors

let us just say what we mean:

i am sorry i made you wait as much as

i am hurt you couldn't

you held my fears over me like

a pendulum for your disposition

(i cannot tell you the forecast i am not a meteorologist)

you accused me of being

confused

you were thinking in twos

planting in soil expecting the sun

entitled to warmth

i am a limited energy source

burnt out

overwatered

(looks like rain again)

does that mean i should never try?

i'm not saying i'm not guilty but i am saying

maybe we want different things

i'm not saying i'm perfect but i am saying

love alone is not enough

and if it was all our problems would have solved themselves

like how
the fact that i needed time
was harder on you than it was on me
maybe it was
(unlike you)
(i cannot read minds or decide what others need)
but i do know
that love is as perennial as the grass
you will find new lovers
who can give you the vulnerability i couldn't
and maybe if i ever feel the pull to try again
(i don't)
(owe you)
(anything)
i will still be young and blossoming
and hopefully we will be watering our gardens
compost making room for things
to bloom
and maybe
it is possible
to reap what you've sewn
and maybe
with love,
in different lots
we can both grow

10,000 leagues
2021

i know it's cliche but i never promised good
just promised myself i'd try and open up
tired metaphor, you, the kind of girl i'd write songs about
the kind of girl they always use the same words for
and even though she can hold her own i think
she deserves more
what about
neon coffin saltwater grave
what about
freckles on your face
jealous of the sun
hot sand cotton warm against your feet
what about
every natural disaster, car crash slapstick synapses
what about
black cat luck, to be magic passing fast through your veins
what about
hard to handle, easy to tame
the k in your name
separates you from the underground
though you like the doors that are closed won't share what's inside
i've pried

i love

your ill-placed commas

our phone calls longer than your wednesday shifts

and the kindness in your paintbrush

you are smart and pretty

you are soft and sweet

you are a surefire storm on the coast

and i am a sailor drowned without hope

i am scared no longer fearful

i am excited no longer exhausted

you are a love song waiting to be written

you are miles and miles of deep blue

see

even if it isn't me

i hope you find somebody that likes exploring

that likes to bowl and watch reality TV

who buys you what i can't afford

and who loves you like i would

maybe better

i haven't even met her

i can't wait to

capricorn lies
8/5/21

today i feel

love in motion

because everything is cause and effect

the nature of the trajectory is such

that i am both fearful and unafraid

ready to risk it all again like i haven't been chewed up and spit out like light at the end of this

supermassive tunnel some kind of

einstein-rosen heartbreak but there's

inertia in her

the kind of pull that creates

binary star systems

she's never been in love

it feels like weightless responsibility

zero gravity pressure

free-fall flowers blooming soundlessly

so i asked myself today

can i really do that?

me?

can i?

and the answer was

with the right person

communication is key
8/31/21

my love

why are you crying like your heart's already broken?

manifest happiness don't steep in self sabotage

thought you said you weren't scared?

doesn't it sting to open up?

doesn't it bruise to lose sleep?

why are you, for the first time,

counting

asking what they had that you didn't

and worrying that you won't?

my love

why are you fretting over mirage

threats

so that just the idea that there could be someone

bigger stronger smarter thinner better

could be hot asphalt on tender skin?

you have walked a long time

now run

don't trip

just fall

heavy
10/27/21

i wonder if regret is genetic

something passed through sequences

like trauma

or a message in a bottle in a lake

with a drowned child resting

under the folds

of the brain

in a quiet mother.

sometimes i wonder

when they will go and how i will feel

and like many others i worry

that the laughter and the limeade

and the orange rolls with the caramel made from white sugar

and the fireworks and parades

were not enough.

Anyway --

i listen to Emma tell me

that since the stroke my grandmother no longer feels like a person

that she still believes she will walk

saves all her best clothes for a special occasion

while grandpa learns how to do the cooking

or asks his daughter to bring something over

Anyway --

i feel like i have missed a boat, not for the first time

sometimes i think

that if i was closer to them

the way i softly simmer at the thought of those whose families are

less like frosted-over freshwater and more like icing on gingerbread,

cooled on racks, while everyone stands in the kitchen and smiles wrinkles into their eyes

Anyway --

maybe it would be harder, then, to see them go

like turning around and missing a wave

or the line for the ferry

(The wait?)

so even though i know it won't be,

i tell myself, maybe it's easier like this

to let the house sink

and leave it there.

3.
2/25/22

do you think that in 2001
our parents thought,
"but it is worse for the children,
to grow up in a world like this."
maybe what they don't know is
everyone who has ever lived
has grown up in this world
and those who haven't
grown up
in a world like this
they are lucky —
no,
maybe there is a better word
to describe them
it is blood-soaked mass-produced
factory paper
this kind of thing which is
indestructible and
impenetrable and
occupational and
imperial and
colonial and

fragile as shrapnel

ripped to shards

rented in shares

they are grown-up and childless

they are wealthy and heartless

i am gasping for breath for my siblings

whose lungs are still growing whose neighbor is death

those who have power have never known life

those who have youth would like to

Turn! Turn! Turn!
5/12/22

Sorry I didn't get back to you I was

Moving forward

Cleo 9-5

Sometime before sunrise

Sorry for the delay I was

Living in the in-between

Seeing new sunsets and sometimes

Taking cover when it rains

(a day in the life)

5/12/22

TUESDAY

the checklist reads:

- ☐ Final exams
- ☐ EMMA CLEO BUREAUCRACY DAY?
- ☐ Frau D. - 15th?
- ☐ Check previous days
- ☐ MyChart - Rx
- ☐ Read lease (1 full month + 1 day) (2 months - good)
- ☐ DJ stuff - Molly & Nate wedding 22nd!
- ☐
- ☐ 2p JUANITA SONITHA SHOWING #207
- ☐ Write living will
- ☐ Translate
- ☐ Post to instagram
- ☐ Clean?
- ☐ Cancel AllState insurance
- ☐ Talk to Tilly
- ☐ Review USTA checklist/reach out to ppl about storage
- ☐ Pack for petsitting - 3 days' clothes + 1 night

i get most things done. i always do.
i am so high-functioning. people barely know

i cry when i work out

i am usually hungry

my brain is always full

that's why i feel like i can't remember anything

that's why i understand when my soulmate arrives

one day early

but i work the next dayand i have a big checklist

lots to remember. no time to cry

so i tell them,

come back tomorrow

when there's less going on

that's when we made plans

so my soulmate leaves.

i get most things done. i always do.

WEDNESDAY

i go to work

i try not to take on too much,

but i still feel anxious when people ask too much of me

i think i expect expectations

isn't that funny?

i think about how sacred laughter is

how i don't do it enough

i take home the pastries when the restaurant closes,

for my neighbors, or for anyone who asks.

i feel very thankful.

missed the bus

but i'm offered a ride home

from there i walk to the liquor store,

to pick up two bottles of wine,

also two cartons of oat milk,

for my soulmate and i, but also for me.

i pass a homeless person

wadded-up dollar bills in my hand,

just in case

he says hello

and introduces himself

his name is tony

and i tell him i'm frankie

and that i will be right back

i run home to get more money, some band-aids, some ibuprofin,

a winter coat

(i forget the water)

i give these things to him and he cries.

he says

"thank you"

he says

"i'm sorry"

we hold hands as he tells me he is so ashamed to be homeless

and i tell him there's nothing he has to be ashamed of.

(i feel ashamed,

of everything i have and forget about, of every life our government has forgotten about,

of a system that has failed the homeless

and allowed police officers to murder unarmed black men,

amongst other things.)

he tells me he wishes he wasn't so old

he tells me when he's rich he'd like to take me out

he tells me he's lonely

his posture is bad his eyes are sorrowful and his heart is so big

that when he says "i love you" i say "i love you, too,

take care, tony"

my soulmate is in the hospital

they didn't ease into the antidepressants

their side effects mimic heart attack symptoms

our plans are canceled

and i find myself wondering whether i should have just invited them in on tuesday

i wonder, if they had died, would i regret sending them away,

with a quick hug and a "text me when you're home safe"

would i regret not making them dinner

right then and there

and put off the things on my to-do list

to just be?

alisa gets home safe eventually.

that night, it storms.

it is the worst storm in a decade.

with ten percent battery i am texting my girlfriend

she is saying she wants to stay together

even though i am leaving for vienna by the end of the summer

the tornado sirens sound,

i think about wet food, wet jackets and wet eyes

and cry when i exercise

the wood floor creaks beneath me

the windows shake and give me shelter

i call up sonny

on facebook video

i open my 2020 wine

and reminisce

while i miss alisa,

i think this is good, too.

i wish there was a word

for that thing that happens

where the world feels like a moment of silence

and joy feels like too much noise

i am holding too much at once

it is spilling over

sonny cries and asks, "why is everything so horrible?"

for all i talk, i can't fill that silence

it echoes like thunder and we are still too afraid to laugh

feeling like it isn't the right time

THURSDAY

i wake up

the sun streams in through my windows

i am thankful that, to my knowledge, no one has died

Today.

i research what to do at a jewish funeral

on my way to buy flowers

only to find out i shouldn't

so i stop at a bakery

to buy some food,

one pastry for each member of the mourning family

of the fatherless son

i add a raspberry passionfruit kouign amann

which i hope declan eats,

because it is exactly the thing i like best.

i didn't know the father.

i had been meaning to meet him.

missed the bus

but i'm offered a ride in the procession

can you imagine running alongside all those cars?

sonny is there

she seems better today

or maybe worse.

the rabbi makes a joke

we laugh

there is something sacred about that

i tear up

when i see the wooden casket

but i stay strong

when i lift the shovel and help bury the body.

they call it chesed shel emet

the ultimate act of kindness.

i tell declan about the kouign amann

and ask everyone for their favorite stories about john,

if only to get to know him a little better

l'chaim!

when i get home,

i take the residence permit application out of my manila folder

and switch to german for two hours

to talk bureaucracy with samanta.

she is very helpful

it comes back immediately, naturally

like riding a bike.

samanta says my german is very good

people won't even know i'm american

i joke that i won't tell them

i'll make them guess

and she says that people might think i'm french

that's how my accent sounds.

i tell her as long as i'm charming and exotic,

i'll make a great first impression

we laugh together

it's a full-bodied thing

i lament the fact that she's getting married

to a wonderful man

and giving away citizenship

that should have been mine.

it's been 10 years

not quite 11

but certainly enough time to imagine being old at the airport

and wishing we were young again.

minutes later,

i join the waiting room for virtual therapy

my therapist says,

"so what would you like to talk about today?"

untitled
6/14/22

dear child,

i hope you live enough summers

to learn in which months the most fragrant trees grow

to recognize which flowers are blooming

and which fruit is in season.

you can pluck it from someone else's yard

i am sure they will have plenty more

dear child,

i hope you take enough sunset walks

to find god

however that manifests,

or to pet at least one dog

and feel the folded petals of a peony

and when petals turn to leaves dry up and frost over,

i hope it is still snowing

so you can hear how still the winter is.

waltz
13.10.22

glossy

oil on canvas

appearing perspiring

klimt quilted

gilded glowing

moon stain

schiele skin of blush and veins

enamoured by your accent

with? prepositioning

coffee stains

wine stains

kiss stains

heartbeats in 3/4

chalk signatures

on my black silk

(pulli?

jumper?

hoody?)

sweat in my shirt as i

gaze into the kind eyes

of the invisible woman who

reminds me too much of a

lover of mine
nein, es tut mir leid
bite-sized goodbyes
youth hostel friends
days so short and nights without end
why can't i explain it
how europe is genuinely
kind and cruel
because time hasn't yet caught up
cozy cool
it reminds me of my family
teaching preaching eating sleeping
what?
you don't care about my rotten teeth?
my selfish genes?
i'll paint over my ancestry
in thick acrylics
until heimat feels like home
until my life feels like vacation
until i never feel alone

VIE
28.1.23

i'm in constant awe of how loved i feel by so many people around me in so many different contexts, so many expansive ways. i am constantly being challenged to love better, to love myself better; constantly i am being shown what it is to be loved, and how colorful this bouquet is, how eclectic its flowers, how tragic and beautiful its blooms, how they carry magic like neutron stars carry mass. that is love so heavy it makes a heart weightless. wir verstehen einander. danke dir.

namenlos
3.1.23

face to face with my own mortality

a gradual, seeping thing

a writhing and weeping seraphim

asks me if i believe in demons

my argument is always that we are inherently good

that babies are born crying because they crave connection

that in unethical or necessary psychological studies they have died without it

and that hate, like common sense, is learned:

but is empathy

enough?

i am a starving vampire

desperate peter pan

i am a lost boy

counting aging women in whose visage i see my mother

coasting the second star to the right running low trying to find fuel

frankl said death is the engine of life

so i put my foot on the gas

the fumes are hedonism the exhaust's cut

i am trying not to care

i am learning how to love

i am dying to keep living

as below, so above

malta
31.3.23

slippery sidewalks

dry white wine

i do things because i don't know when i will do them next

i don't know if i am in love,

but isn't it enough?

maybe i need someone simple

someone easy

no one to complicate things to twist my words or challenge my touch

i live my life like intuition

bus 222 a rickety rollercoaster

hitting the brakes when i'm too many drinks in

i feel rich

maybe i don't have prada or a private jet

but i can buy gelato, isn't that enough?

BER
07.04.23

a berlin cold & dreary

you are like squares and shapes

primary colors

thick paints and concrete plastik beton

sculpted

from a weimar goldmine leveled

by bombs & bauhaus

train tracks and sticky subways

lead to knowhere

somewhere filthy

somewhere fine

somewhere yours

somewhere mine

ab und zu
10.4.23

the soreness between my thighs

is nothing compared to the ache in my heart

you put it there

after all these years,

i am still afraid to fall in love

i am not used to being taken care of

i am not used to being held

by strangers in berlin clubs

who count the seconds softly who tell me they believe in me

old men with bubble holsters on kinky techno soap floors pulsating vibrating vitality

inspire me to grow and age

that my body must decay in nebulae

uterusless and birthing stars in brilliant blooming pain

that my body reminds me of its cosmic capacity

is that zeit / geistig

i am not sure

i only know the enamel deliciously dissolving from hand-rolled lollipops sucked on the subway

you fucked me over the couch you always make sure i come first

sugar kisses on the comedown

i thought i wanted objectification

insidious intentions permeating penetrating paid for their stupid expensive wine the name of my ex the one with the k until i experienced it

i thought i wanted intellectualization

theorizing academicizing ostracizing dialectics exclusionary politics definition gestalt relativism i went on and on

until the stop where

i fell asleep in your arms while you pet my hair

upon arrival

i woke up burning in starlight and longitudinal waves

i thought i wanted to be alone

but with you, it's easy

inland/ausland

30.5.23

as dew begins to form

and the streets begin to smell again

and flora blooms looming in the narrow patches slammed between concrete blocks

draped in ornate dulcet window frames

that project sunlight stains onto their neighbors

whose windows are too close --

i become less like a tourist

and more like an attraction,

a fixture in the architecture,

a person in the background of a photo

buying groceries

and making appointments

to have the fridge fixed --

and i buy the produce daily

and partake too often in bread

and take too many naps

never quite a permanent structure,

i renew my lease

on belonging

to a city which quietly broke my heart

with building block language

while my own native tongue

fell so fluidly in love

and my mouth stretched itself like clay over her body

catching feelings / nothing to hide
8/21/23

it wasn't a date

came back stateside for a while

stumbled down the stairs into the beat and found him at the bar where he asked for a hug and i gave him a little more

crashed his afterparty where he showed me the studio why he kissed me goodbye i still don't know

the first date

fell into bed with me

ephemeral euphoria

whispered he was falling for me

on the second date

on the dancefloor he was steady on his feet when he called me baby and asked me not to kiss him in public

we swayed seven miles away

while he caught up with his friends

i wonder what is so shameful about me

that he can breathe out praises against my lips

find nirvana between my thighs

and then tell me i'm not his secret while he hides me from inquiring minds

by the third date

i want someone to take me out and show me off

follow me across oceans in a private jet

and in my honor compose a set

that i can close my eyes to

when i start feeling too good

transitions (feat. U & I)
8/24/23

i want that heavy rhythm and those off-beat vocals (rest)

i want flats and sharps; strings and tambourines (rest)

i want bass that makes my heart feel like it's beating again (rest)

1 2 3 4

light refracts across every surface of the insides of me (rest)

i am visceral and finally fearless (rest)

i break my heart and fall in love daily (rest) i can break yours too if you want

5 6 7 8

last night i dreamed i left a suitcase here

i have no time to (rest)

i am frantic i am hungry

i dress myself and (dance)

as if it will stretch the sound

just a little farthermargaux pas nouveaux pas 2023

servers show up set up for success

to satiate their uninhibited thirst

and unpowdered noses

septums pierced and sobbing in the freezer

house shakes on the weekend

body aches, sexed and satiated

fucked and feeling too much

let go let go let go

don't take it home with you

just take me home

stop resting for tomorrow's hustle

and start losing sleep for the heart & soul

love letter to lucy & friends
00:00

are you ready? no? okay, here we go!

the only wrong way to do it is to try and control it

get on the bus, don't worry who's driving

rollercoaster climb on a highway to heaven

hold your hands up, enjoy the ride!

we'll be here for a while

we'll be here for an inch, we'll be here for a mile

what a gift it is to see things as they are

what a gift it is to be seen

without asking, "how do i look?"

what a gift it is to share consciousness

to peer into reality for one eternal moment

to find the isness of everything, to know the meaning of words without language

peacock feathers, soapy edges softening, fractal melody

coming back to a world where time is a boundary where parameters imprison

time to pretend i never left

time to pretend

how

to

know time!

MDMA
00:00

i can feel the neurogenesis
i want to love you like a partner
want to hold you like a lover
and show you what plato really meant
we can transcend
i would say the same things sober
i know at some point it's all over
but right now we are right here
i would like to split myself open
and peel back the layers
like a nesting doll
at the center, desire
connection a non-material item
collecting dust in thick layers of mass-produced monetization
wipe it off and keep scrubbing
i want to see you without makeup
i want to take off your mask
can i? tell me to stop and i will
hesitation a learned mechanism suffocating innate noise
we cry to communicate
comedowns softened by warm arms and hands
i am so cold but i am learning how to be
rose petal fragile

chaleur humaine

9/10/23

i feel the quiet cacophony

of centuries of laughter in the middle of blood-soaked battlefields

it settles over me

like a thick coat of snow on tired autumn's growth

i feel the morning sunlight

hot on ancient foundations

brick mortar sweat and tears

shakes heaven's firmaments like hell's enticing thunder

somewhere a baby is born

eyes opening wet and sticky and filled with stars

at the same time a grandfather fits his bracelet into the hand of a grandson which closes around it his only memento of war fought and in whose name

dead light shines slow and far

we have loved

as deeply as fiercely as long as we have grieved

at the same time

a shaky exhale out

a gasp in

sun sets

on the horizon

flowers rise

F.S. Withers was born in Minneapolis, Minnesota, and graduated from the University of Minnesota with a degree in Psychology and German, respectively. They have been writing poetry since they were a child and prior to this publication their writing has appeared only in small academic collections. Mx. Withers came out as pansexual in 2008 and as nonbinary in 2013 and considers queerness inseparable from poetry. In 2022, Mx. Withers left their life behind to teach English in Vienna, Austria, where they continue to be inspired.

www.ingramcontent.com/pod-product-compliance
Lightning Source LLC
Chambersburg PA
CBHW052205070526
44585CB00017B/2081